GET
SH*T
DONE

Edited by Lauris Liberts &
STARTUPVITAMINS

PORTFOLIO
PENGUIN

PORTFOLIO / PENGUIN

Published by the Penguin Group

Penguin Group (USA) LLC
375 Hudson Street
New York, New York 10014

USA | Canada | UK | Ireland | Australia | New Zealand | India |
South Africa | China

penguin.com

A Penguin Random House Company

First published by Portfolio / Penguin, a member of Penguin
Group (USA) LLC, 2014

Copyright © 2014 by Idea Bits, LLC

ISBN 978-1-59184-764-9

Printed in China

10 9 8 7 6 5 4 3 2 1

Set in Museo Sans, Archer, Univers, Trend Slab, DINPro and
DINfun Pro

CONTENTS

1.

GET SH*I*T
DONE

#001

GET SHIT
DONE.

Aaron Levie, Box

#GET**SHIT**DONE

#002

LESS MEETINGS MORE DOING

Jason Goldberg, Fab.com

#003

PERFECTIONISM IS OFTEN AN EXCUSE FOR PROCRASTINATION.

Paul Graham, Y Combinator

#004

DO, OR DO NOT. THERE IS ~~NO TRY~~.

Yoda

#005

My best entrepreneurial
advice is **to start.**

Dave Morin, Path

#006

You don't need **more time,**
you just need **to decide.**

Seth Godin

YOU CAN'T BUILD A REPUTATION ON WHAT YOU ARE GOING TO DO.

Henry Ford

#008

OPTIMISM,
PESSIMISM,
FUCK THAT;
WE'RE GOING TO
MAKE IT HAPPEN.

Elon Musk, Tesla Motors

#GET**SHIT**DONE

#009

You can't be that kid standing
at the top of the waterslide,
overthinking it. You have
to go down the chute.

Tina Fey

#010

Life is short. Do stuff that matters.

Siqi Chen, Hey Inc.

#011

Don't
compromise.

Steve Jobs

#012

Some people
<u>want it</u> to happen,
some <u>wish it</u> would happen,
others <u>make it</u> happen.

Michael Jordan

Don't spend so much time trying to **choose** the perfect opportunity, that you miss the right opportunity.

Michael Dell

#014

NEVER HALF-ASS
TWO THINGS.☒☒
WHOLE-ASS
ONE THING.☑

Ron Swanson, Parks and Recreation

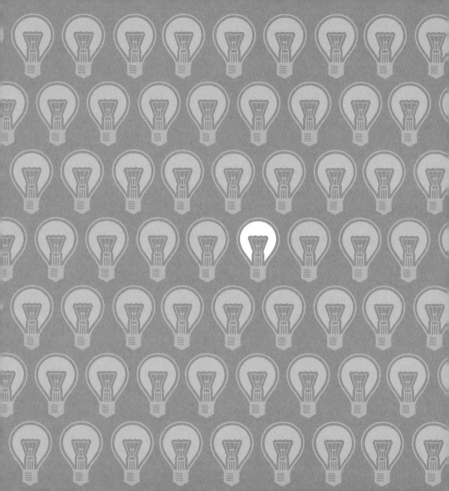

2.

THINK

#015

THINK
BIGGER.

Tony Hsieh, Zappos.com

#THINK

#016

BE AMAZING.
BE REVOLUTIONARY.

Blake Mycoskie, TOMS Shoes

#THINK

#017

Lives Remaining:

ZERO.

Alexis Ohanian, Reddit

#THINK

Innovation is hard because *'solving problems people didn't know they had'* and *'building something no one needs'* look identical at first.

Aaron Levie, Box

#019

ALWAYS CHALLENGE
the *old* ways.

Howard Schultz, Starbucks

#THINK

#020

Your margin is
MY OPPORTUNITY.

Jeff Bezos, Amazon

#021

Passion
never fails.

Paul Chen, FloNetwork, Fortiva

#THINK

#022

Luck
is what happens when
preparation meets opportunity.

Seneca

#THINK

#023

**CHASE THE VISION,
NOT THE MONEY;**
the money will end up
following you.

Tony Hsieh, Zappos.com

#THINK

#024

Ideas are like **RABBITS**.
You get a couple and
learn how to handle them,
and pretty soon you have
a dozen.

John Steinbeck

#THINK

#025

Great companies
don't throw *money* at problems,
they throw *ideas* at problems.

Greg McAdoo, Sequoia Capital

#THINK

#026

Most of entrepreneurship
is differentiating between
*good-
sounding* and *dumb-
sounding*
dumb ideas ⟵ *good ideas.*

Aaron Gotwalt, CoTweet, Seesaw
Decisions

#THINK

#027

Entrepreneur
is just French for
'has ideas, does them'.

Alexis Ohanian, Reddit

#THINK

#028

Ideas are worthless
until you get them
out of your head to
see what they can do.

Tanner Christensen,
creative strategist

#THINK

#029

Most people think
it's all about the idea.
IT'S NOT.

Everyone has ideas...
The hard part is to
execute on the idea.

Mark Cuban

#THINK

#030

SIMPLE

can be harder than
COMPLEX.

You have to work hard
to get your thinking
clean to make it simple.

Steve Jobs

#THINK

It's hard to do a really good job on anything you don't think about in the shower.

Paul Graham, Y Combinator

#THINK

#032

The risk is not
in doing something
that feels risky.
The risk is in not doing
something that feels risky.

Andy Dunn, Bonobos

#THINK

It's not about the amount
of wealth you can accumulate,
**it's about the impact
and change you can create.**

Neil Blumenthal, Warby Parker

#034

People can copy
what you've done,
but they can't copy
what you're going to do.

Dennis Crowley, Foursquare

OPPORTUNITY
lives at the intersection
of what people need tomorrow
and can be just barely built today.

Aaron Levie, Box

#036

Embrace what you don't know,
especially in the beginning
because what you don't know
can become your greatest asset.
It ensures that you will
absolutely be doing things
different from everybody else.

Sara Blakely, Spanx

#THINK

#037

[The] best startups
generally come from
somebody needing to
SCRATCH AN ITCH.

Michael Arrington, TechCrunch

#THINK

#038

Start with the assumption
that the best way to do
something is not the way
it's being done right now.

Aaron Levie, Box

#THINK

#039

Optimism

should be at the top of an entrepreneur's checklist.

Alana Muller, Kauffman FastTrac

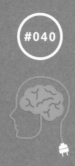

#040

Man's mind, once stretched
by a new idea, never regains
its original dimensions.

Oliver Wendell Holmes

#THINK

#041

EVEN IF YOU DON'T HAVE THE PERFECT IDEA TO BEGIN WITH, YOU CAN LIKELY ADAPT.

Victoria Ransom, Wildfire

#042

THE FASTEST WAY TO CHANGE YOURSELF IS TO HANG OUT WITH PEOPLE WHO ARE ALREADY THE WAY YOU WANT TO BE.

Reid Hoffman, LinkedIn

#THINK

#043

Don't play games
that you don't understand,
even if you see lots of
other people making
money from them.

Tony Hsieh, Zappos.com

#THINK

#044

We should call
them createups,
NOT STARTUPS.
The goal is not to
start something,
the goal is to
create something.

Dharmesh Shah, HubSpot

#THINK

#045

You can't put
out projects
that you don't
use yourself.

Gary Vaynerchuk, VaynerMedia

#THINK

#046

A pessimist sees the difficulty in every opportunity; an optimist sees the opportunity in every difficulty.

Winston Churchill

#047

The task we must
set for ourselves is
not to feel secure,
but to be able to
tolerate insecurity.

Erich Fromm

#THINK

#048

Openly share and talk
to people about your idea.
Use their lack of interest or
doubt to fuel your motivation
to make it happen.

Todd Garland, BuySellAds

#049

You should set goals
beyond your reach
so you *always have
something to live for.*

Ted Turner, TBS, CNN

#THINK

#050

The difference between a vision and a hallucination is that *other people can see the vision.*

Marc Andreessen,
Andreessen Horowitz

#THINK

PLAN

#051

Quality
is the <u>best</u> business plan.

John Lasseter, Pixar

#PLAN

#052

The <u>first</u> draft of anything
is shit.

Ernest Hemingway

#PLAN

#053

A good plan,
violently executed **NOW**,
is better than a perfect plan
NEXT WEEK.

General George Patton

#PLAN

#054

We don't always know
what's going to happen.
And that's **OK.**

Biz Stone, Twitter

#055

Advice for young entrepreneurs – unproven ideas and people are OK, stick to proven business models though.

James Tudsbury,
Monster Digital Marketing

#PLAN

#056

PROJECTIONS ARE BULLSHIT. THEY'RE JUST GUESSES.

Jason Fried, 37Signals

#057

Building a successful
business model
isn't about changing your
company based on every
bit of feedback:
*It's about understanding
whom to listen to and why.*

Steve Blank, E.piphany

#PLAN

Don't spend too
much time planning,
release early and often, some
things will work, others won't,
refine and move forward
and above all forget the money,
*just make sure you love
what you're doing.*

Kevin Rose, Digg, Revision3

#PLAN

#059

STAY SELF-FUNDED AS LONG AS POSSIBLE.

Garrett Camp, Expa,
Uber and StumbleUpon

If you prematurely invest
all your time and money
on the wrong idea, you have
nothing left to try new ideas.

Alberto Savoia

BUILD

#061

IF YOU CAN'T EXPLAIN IT SIMPLY, YOU DON'T UNDERSTAND IT WELL ENOUGH

Albert Einstein

#BUILD

#062

IDEAS ARE EASY. IMPLEMENTATION IS HARD.

Guy Kawasaki

#063

You jump off a cliff
and you assemble an
airplane on the way down.

Reid Hoffman, LinkedIn

#BUILD

The great thing about taking big chances when you're younger is you have less to lose and you don't know as much. So you <u>take big swings</u>.

Amy Poehler

#065

A GOOD DESIGNER

finds an elegant way to put
everything you need on a page.

A GREAT DESIGNER

convinces you half that
shit is unnecessary.

Mike Monteiro, art designer
and director

#BUILD

Launching a startup
is like firing off a rocket ship,
then trying to hold it
together with duct tape.

Shane Snow, Contently

#BUILD

STOP SKETCHING. START BUILDING.

Dennis Crowley, Foursquare

#BUILD

#068

MAKE SOMETHING PEOPLE WANT.

Paul Graham, Y Combinator

#069

Waiting for perfect is never as smart as making progress.

Seth Godin

#BUILD

#070

Socrates said,
'Know thyself.'
I say,
'Know thy users.'

Joshua Brewer, Twitter

#BUILD

#071

What will **BLOW**
our customers' minds?

Aaron Levie, Box

#BUILD

#072

Always deliver
MORE than expected.

Larry Page, Google

#073

Fuck it.
Ship it.

Betaworks

#BUILD

Quality is more important than quantity.
One home run is much better than two doubles.

Steve Jobs

#075

Obsess about the

QUALITY

of the product.

Sam Altman, Y Combinator

#BUILD

BE NARROW.

It's much better to mean a great deal to a few people than next to nothing to a huge amount.

David Hieatt, Hiut Denim

#BUILD

Perfection is achieved, *not when there is nothing more to add*, but when there is *nothing left to take away*.

Antoine de Saint-Exupéry

#BUILD

Creative process:
1. This is going to be awesome.
2. This is hard.
3. This is terrible.
4. I'm terrible.
5. Hey, not bad.
6. That was awesome.

Kazu Kibuishi, Flight, Copper

I don't know the key to success, but the key to failure is trying to please everyone.

Bill Cosby

#080

Minimize complexity.
The simpler the product,
the more likely you are
to actually ship it,
and the more likely you are
to fix problems quickly.

Slava Akhmechet, RethinkDB

#BUILD

MINIMALISM

is not a *lack* of something.
It's simply the
perfect amount of something.

Nicholas Burroughs, designer

#082

Not having a clear goal
**LEADS TO DEATH
BY A THOUSAND
COMPROMISES.**

Mark Pincus, Zynga

Focusing on
one thing and doing
it really, really well
can get you <u>very far</u>.

Kevin Systrom, Instagram

#BUILD

#084

If you are not embarrassed
by the first version
of your product,
you've launched too late.

Reid Hoffman, LinkedIn

#BUILD

#085

The longer it takes to develop, the less likely it is to launch.

Jason Fried, 37Signals

#BUILD

Metrics are for doing,
not for staring.
Never measure
just because you can.
Measure to learn.
Measure to fix.

Stijn Debrouwere, journalist

#BUILD

#087

Human nature has a tendency
to *admire complexity*,
but *reward simplicity*.

Ben Huh,
The Cheezburger Network

#088

User experience matters a lot.
More than most people realize.
The best-designed user
experiences get out of the
way and just help people
get shit done. Less is more.
If you have to explain it,
you've already failed.

Jason Goldberg, Fab.com

#BUILD

#089

Remember that you are more likely to die because you execute badly than get crushed by a competitor.

Sam Altman, Y Combinator

#BUILD

#090

You have to make
every single detail

PERFECT.

And you have to limit
the number of details.

Jack Dorsey, Twitter

#BUILD

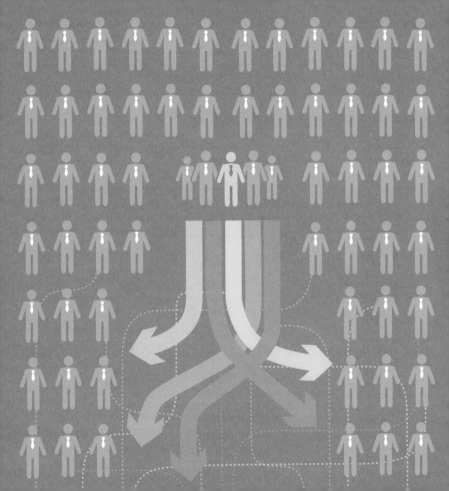

5.

LEAD

#091

IF EVERYTHING
SEEMS UNDER CONTROL
YOU'RE JUST NOT
GOING FAST ENOUGH.

Mario Andretti, racing driver

#LEAD

#092

Startups must have a
'True North',
a destination in mind.
That vision must be
constant and powerful.

Eric Ries, The Lean Startup

#LEAD

#093

Start your business
by doing every job yourself.
It's the only way to learn what
you need and who will then
be best able to do it for you.

Danielle Newnham, We Make Play

#LEAD

#094

An entrepreneur
isn't someone who owns
a business, it's someone
who makes things happen.

Tim Ferriss

#095

A *real* entrepreneur
is somebody who has
NO SAFETY NET
underneath them.

Henry Kravis,
Kohlberg Kravis Roberts & Co.

#LEAD

If you're not nervous about one or two decisions every day, you probably aren't trying hard enough.

Tim O'Shaughnessy, LivingSocial

#LEAD

Hire character. Train skill.

Peter Schutz, Porsche

#098

You know you've
done something **right**
when everyone else at
the conference table
is smarter than you.

Chuck Gordon, SpareFoot

#LEAD

No man will make a great leader who wants *to do it all himself* or *get all the credit for doing it.*

Andrew Carnegie

#100

There's nothing wrong with staying small. You can do

BIG THINGS

with a

SMALL TEAM.

Jason Fried, 37Signals

#LEAD

#101

COMPLAINING
IS NOT
A STRATEGY.

Jeff Bezos, Amazon

#102

GREAT COMPANIES ARE BUILT, NOT LAUNCHED.

Robert Scoble, Scobleizer

Don't forget that if slowness is a bug, then speed is absolutely a feature.

Eric Feng, Flipboard

Managers tell you where you are, leaders tell you where you're going.

Michael Lopp, author

#105

Always treat your employees
exactly as you want them
to treat your best customers.

Stephen R. Covey

BE MORE TOLERANT OF THE DIFFICULT PEOPLE.

They're the creative ones.
They're not happy with
the status quo.

Terry Leahy, Tesco

You have to have *more leadership, less management.* It's about getting stuff done. You can sit around and analyze things forever but while you do that the competition has moved on.

Peter Vesterbacka, Rovio, Angry Birds

#108

Do your homework and know your business better than anyone. Otherwise, someone who knows more and works harder will **KICK YOUR ASS.**

Mark Cuban

#109

Often, the best companies
are ones where the product
is an extension of the
founder's personality.

Naval Ravikant, AngelList,
Venture Hacks

Entrepreneurship
is not a part-time job, and
it's not even a full-time job.
It's a lifestyle.

Carrie Layne, BestBuzz

#111

Running a startup is like being punched in the face repeatedly, but working for a large company is like being water-boarded.

Paul Graham, Y Combinator

#LEAD

#112

You cannot
mandate productivity,
you must provide the tools to
let people become their best.

Steve Jobs

#113

It helps not to call people *'human resources'*. They're people. And, as it turns out, people like to be treated like people.
Go figure.

Dharmesh Shah, HubSpot

#LEAD

#114

If you *don't have
people that care about
usability on your project,*
your project is doomed.

Jeff Atwood, Stack Overflow

#115

Good products are built by people who want to use it themselves.

David Karp, Tumblr

#LEAD

#116

Don't be a complainer;
make things better,
let it go, or take action
to make it better.

Tina Roth Eisenberg, Tattly

#117

A GREAT PRODUCT
MANAGER

has the brain of an engineer,
the heart of a designer, and
the speech of a diplomat.

Deep Nishar, LinkedIn

#LEAD

#118

SHARE RESULTS
(financial and key metrics)
with the company
every month.

Sam Altman, Y Combinator

#119

WHEN YOU'RE A ONE-MAN SHOW YOU HAVE TO FOCUS ON THE MOST IMPORTANT THING TO GET DONE TODAY.

Noah Everett, Twitpic

#LEAD

#120

LIFE OF AN ENTREPRENEUR: I WAKE UP EXCITED AND TERRIFIED EVERY DAY.

Sarah Lacy, PandoDaily

#LEAD

6.

$ELL

#121

Your brand is what other
people say about you
when you're *not* in the room.

Jeff Bezos, Amazon

There is only *one* boss.
The customer.
And he can fire everybody
in the company from
the chairman on down,
simply by spending his
money somewhere else.

Sam Walton, Wal-Mart

Treat your customers like they *own you.* Because they do.

Mark Cuban

The customer isn't *always* right.
But if you *don't* listen
to them, your product
won't be either.

Oli Gardner, Unbounce

#125

Care about your customers
more than about yourself,
and you'll do well.

Derek Sivers, CD Baby

Sales go up and down, SERVICE STAYS FOREVER.

Jason Goldberg, Fab.com

#SELL

#127

Our job is not to please investors. Our job is to delight our users.

Micki Krimmel, Neighborgoods

#128

It's better to have a few users love your product than for a lot of users to sort of like it.

Sam Altman, Y Combinator

#SELL

#129

You can't just ask customers
what they want and then
try to give that to them.
By the time you get it built,
they'll want something new.

Steve Jobs

#SELL

The path to greatness is rarely having the best technology. It is far more often having the better relationship with the customer. It is a marketing game – not a technology game.

Joseph Barisonzi, Strategic Growth Initiative, CommunityLeader

#131

NOTHING INFLUENCES
PEOPLE MORE THAN
A RECOMMENDATION
FROM A TRUSTED FRIEND.

Mark Zuckerberg

#SELL

INVESTORS, MOST OF THEM, HAVE A HERD MENTALITY. THEY WANT TO INVEST ONLY IF OTHER PEOPLE ARE INVESTING.

Jessica Livingston, Y Combinator

7

PERSEVERE

#133

THE HARD PART
IS WHAT SEPARATES
GOOD FROM GREAT.

Noah Kagan, AppSumo

#PERSEVERE

#134

FIND YOUR ONE THING AND DO THAT ONE THING BETTER THAN ANYONE ELSE.

Jason Goldberg, Fab.com

#PERSEVERE

Costs are like fingernails. You have to cut them constantly.

Carlos Alberto Sicupira,
Anheuser-Busch InBev

#136

When you're small, being *faster* than your competitors is your biggest and sometimes <u>only advantage</u>.

Eric Ryan and Adam Lowry,
The Method Method

#PERSEVERE

Your work is going to
fill a large part of your life,
and the only way to be truly
satisfied is to do what you
believe is great work. And the
only way to do great work is to
love what you do.

Steve Jobs

#PERSEVERE

Hard work
is *always* the difference
between opportunities.

Eric Rewitzer, 3Fish Studios

#PERSEVERE

#139

Under pressure,
you don't rise to the
occasion, you *sink* to
the level of your training.
That's why we train so hard.

A Navy SEAL

I never took a day off
in my twenties.
NOT ONE.

Bill Gates

Don't worry about failure;
you only have to be right
ONCE.

Drew Houston, Dropbox

SUCCESS IS NEVER GETTING TO THE BOTTOM OF YOUR TO-DO LIST.

Marissa Mayer, Yahoo

#PERSEVERE

It takes time, it's a grind.
There are *no* shortcuts.
You've got to
GRIND and GRIND.

Mark Cuban

#144

The difference in winning & losing is, most often, **NOT QUITTING**.

Walt Disney

#PERSEVERE

Timing, perseverance,
and ten years of trying will
eventually make you look
like an overnight success.

Biz Stone, Twitter

Don't let people tell you your ideas won't work. If you're passionate about an idea that's stuck in your head, find a way to build it so you can prove to yourself that it doesn't work.

Dennis Crowley, Foursquare

#PERSEVERE

#147

If you never want to be criticized, for goodness' sake don't do anything new.

Jeff Bezos, Amazon

#PERSEVERE

#148

There are lots of ways
for investors to say no to you,
and I'm pretty sure I've heard
every single one.

Ben Silbermann, Pinterest

#PERSEVERE

#149

Sleep

is that time
you're working on startup
problems with your
eyes closed.

Dharmesh Shah, HubSpot

#PERSEVERE

#150

The number-one determinant of entrepreneurial success is persistence. If you are not prepared to go to **SUPERHUMAN** levels that are beyond rationality to realize your dream, then your chance of finding success is virtually *ZERO*.

Chris Barton, Shazam

#PERSEVERE

#151

When you innovate,
you've got to be prepared
for people telling you that
you are nuts.

Larry Ellison, Oracle

#152

Most people are searching
for a path to success that
is both easy and certain.
Most paths are neither.

Seth Godin

#153

Your biggest challenge as an entrepreneur is not concealing your idea from others or keeping your idea a secret, it is actually convincing people that you're not crazy and that you can pull this off.

Sean Parker, Napster

Almost everything important is at first opposed by stakeholders in the status quo. Be *relentless, persistent* and *tenacious.*

Steve Blank, E.piphany

#PERSEVERE

IT ALWAYS <u>TAKES</u> TWICE AS LONG AND <u>COSTS</u> TWICE AS MUCH.

Cyrus Vance,
former US Secretary of State

#PERSEVERE

#156

'EASY'
is a word that's used to
describe *other people's* jobs.

Jason Fried, 37Signals

All that matters in business is that you get it right once. Then everyone can tell you how lucky you are.

Mark Cuban

#158

As your audience grows, the chance of any given action triggering criticism asymptotically approaches 100 percent.

Allen Pike, app designer

8.

EVOLVE

#159

I have not failed.
I've just found 10,000
ways that won't work.

Thomas Edison

#160

In business by the time you realize you're in trouble, it's too late to save yourself. Unless you're running scared all the time, you're gone.

Bill Gates

#161

Make something someone
specific needs, launch fast,
let users show you what
to change, change it,
repeat last two.

Paul Graham, Y Combinator

#EVOLVE

#162

IDENTIFY YOUR PROBLEMS BUT GIVE YOUR POWER AND ENERGY TO SOLUTIONS.

Tony Robbins

#163

The pivot.

It used to be called, 'the fuck-up'.

Marc Andreessen,
Andreessen Horowitz

#164

It is easier to recognize other people's mistakes than *our own.* Always ask for feedback.

@Expa

#165

It was *very easy*
to be DIFFERENT,
but *very difficult*
to be BETTER.

Jony Ive, Apple

#166

Failure is not the *opposite* of success
BUT A STEPPING
STONE TO SUCCESS.

Arianna Huffington

Nothing works better than just *improving* your product.

Joel Spolsky, Stack Exchange

#168

If you do something
and it turns out pretty good,
then you should go do
something else wonderful,
not dwell on it for too long.
Just figure out what's next.

Steve Jobs

#EVOLVE

For every new feature we add,
we take an old one out.
A lot of big sites don't do that,
and it's a problem.

David Karp, Tumblr

Don't be dismissive of criticism.
Instead, use it to improve your
product. Your most vocal critics
will often turn into your biggest
champions if you take their
criticism seriously.

Slava Akhmechet, RethinkDB

#171

YESTERDAY'S HOME RUNS **DON'T WIN** TODAY'S GAMES.

Babe Ruth

#172

YOUR MOST
UNHAPPY
CUSTOMERS ARE YOUR
GREATEST SOURCE OF
LEARNING.

Bill Gates

#EVOLVE

Anyone who stops learning
is old, whether at twenty
or eighty. Anyone who
keeps learning stays young.
The greatest thing in life
is to keep your mind young.

Henry Ford